HEALTH ISSUES

DYSLEXIA

Paula Wiltshire

HODDER
Wayland

an imprint of Hodder Children's Books

White-Thomson Publishing Ltd,
2-3 St Andrew's Place, Lewes,
East Sussex BN7 1UP

Published in Great Britain in 2002 by Hodder
Wayland, an imprint of Hodder Children's
Books.

Reprinted in 2003

This book was produced for White-Thomson
Publishing Ltd by Ruth Nason.

Design: Carole Binding
Picture research: Glass Onion Pictures

British Library Cataloguing in Publication Data
Wiltshire, Paula
    Dyslexia. - (Health Issues)
    1. Dyslexia - Juvenile literature
    I. Title II. Nason, Ruth
    616.8'5'53

ISBN 0 7502 3947 6

Printed in Hong Kong by Wing King Tong.

Hodder Children's Books
A division of Hodder Headline Limited
338 Euston Road, London NW1 3BH

Acknowledgements
The author and publishers thank the following for their permission to reproduce photographs and
illustrations: British Museum: page 26; Camera Press: page 17; Martyn Chillmaid: pages 11, 18, 21,
22, 27, 36, 40, 43, 49, 51, 52, 53, 56, 58l, 58r; Corbis Images: pages 4t (Bob Rowan; Progressive
Images), 8, 9 (Bettmann), 19 (Robert Maass), 28 (Dave Bartruff), 35 (Allana Wesley White), 55 (Bruce
Burkhardt); imagingbody.com: pages 4b, 6, 10, 14, 31, 41; Impact: pages 24 (Peter Arkell), 33 (Peter
Arkell), 57 (Bruce Stephens); Mediscan: cover and pages 1 and 7; Photofusion: pages 59l (Gina
Glover), 59r (Bob Watkins); Popperfoto: pages 15, 25, 32, 48; Science Photo Library: page 13 (Eye of
Science); Scottish Viewpoint: pages 47l, 50; Topham Picturepoint: page 16. The photos on pages 12,
37, 38 and 44 are from the Wayland Picture Library. The illustrations on pages 23, 29, 39, 42, 45
and 54 are by Carole Binding.

Thanks are also due to the following people for their help and co-operation: Dr Albert Galaburda,
Gerri Morris, Jane Orr, Carol Orton, Hazel Richardson, Robin Salter, Christine Schick, Ian Smythe.

Note: Photographs illustrating the case studies in this book were posed by models.

Contents

Introduction
What is dyslexia?

Dyslexia is a learning difficulty that is thought to affect between 8 and 10 per cent of the population in the Western world. Researchers estimate that 2-4 per cent of the population are severely affected, while the rest of the people with dyslexia have mild to moderate problems. So, in every class of twenty-five students, two or three are probably affected by dyslexia to some extent.

Reading and writing

Reading, writing and spelling are the main skills affected by dyslexia.

Jo's new ambition

Jo remembers how she muddled through as a dyslexic teenager: 'In the end I hardly used to go to school. It didn't seem worth it. I wasn't learning anything. I had a part-time job at the local hairdresser's and, when I was old enough, they took me on full time. I got to know where everything was and everyone knew it was difficult for me with the appointments and the formulas, but it didn't worry them; they helped me out. It was comfortable working there and I enjoyed talking to the clients and listening to their problems. Even though it wasn't really stretching me, I could probably have stayed there for years.

The problem was, I got sick to death of eating omelettes! Every time I went out for a meal, I would pretend that I was a really fussy eater, because I couldn't actually read the menu. I'd pretend to look at it and then I'd say, "I think I'd better just stick to a plain omelette." Friends thought I was really boring and unadventurous but, actually, I was just scared of being found out.'

Now life is different for Jo. She is attending a special adult dyslexia unit at her local college, to improve her literacy. She hopes to go on to university and become a social worker.

Myths about dyslexia

- *Dyslexia is just an excuse for being dumb.*
- *Dyslexia doesn't really exist – it's made up by parents who can't face the fact that their kid isn't very bright.*
- *All dyslexic people are highly intelligent.*
- *Dyslexia only affects boys.*
- *All dyslexic people are very creative.*
- *If you're dyslexic you'll never be able to read or write.*
- *You can't be dyslexic if you **can** read and write.*
- *Dyslexics are just plain lazy.*

Truths about dyslexia

- *Dyslexia affects people of all intellectual abilities.*
- *It affects both boys and girls.*
- *It varies in degree from person to person. Some people are severely affected and find it very difficult to read and write. Others have university degrees.*
- *Like every person in the world, each dyslexic person is unique and individual in their pattern of strengths and difficulties.*
- *Dyslexia affects people from all backgrounds.*
- *Dyslexic people **always** have strengths in some areas and these often come out as creative talents.*
- *Because of the way their brains process information, dyslexic people can often see situations differently and find unusual ways of solving problems.*
- *Dyslexic people of all ages can learn effectively, but may need to be taught using multisensory methods (see Chapter 3).*
- *A dyslexic student probably has to work at least twice as hard as a non-dyslexic student to produce the same standard of work.*

The word 'dyslexia' comes from Greek and means 'faulty' or 'difficult' (*dys*) and 'words' (*lexia*). Dyslexia affects a person's ability to read, write and spell and, sometimes, understand numbers and maths. It can also cause problems with understanding the difference between directions, such as left and right and east and west; remembering lists of items; and putting things in sequence, such as the alphabet or months of the year. It can cause difficulty with understanding the passing of time. All of these can have a devastating effect on a person's everyday life. Throughout this book we will be hearing from people of all ages who are dyslexic. They will share some of the difficulties they have encountered and, also, some of the strategies they have used to overcome their problems.

'This guy started shouting, "Are you stupid or something? Can't you read?" I looked up and everyone was staring at me. I was so embarrassed. I just wanted to die.'
(Paul, aged 15)

Dyslexia has been called the 'hidden disability', because it's impossible to tell whether or not someone is dyslexic simply by looking at them. A dyslexic person does not carry a white stick and yet they may not be able to read notices or signs any more than someone who is visually impaired.

What causes dyslexia?

There are many theories as to why some people are dyslexic and we will look at these in more detail in Chapter 1. The most popular theory at the moment is that dyslexia could be caused by a combination of biological factors. These are things that happen in our bodies. Researchers are looking at how the dyslexic brain works, using MRI (Magnetic Resonance Imaging) scanners. Scientists are also studying whether or not dyslexia is inherited.

Getting around
Having difficulty reading signs at an airport or station can spoil the enjoyment of travelling.

About this book

Many dyslexic people are ashamed of the fact that they find it difficult to read or write, because of the way other people judge them or make jokes about them. The aim of this book is to dispel the myths about dyslexia and address some of the issues that can arise. Chapter 2 looks at the signs to look out for if someone thinks they may be dyslexic and how they would go about being assessed. In

Chapter 3 we'll look at how dyslexia affects reading and writing both at school and in everyday life, and in Chapter 4 we'll consider the other areas that can be affected by dyslexia, such as maths, music, foreign languages and organizational skills. We'll also see some ways in which people have overcome problems in these areas.

Exams are often a difficult time for dyslexic students, so Chapter 5 looks at ways in which they can learn and revise more effectively. Throughout the book we'll look at how the family and friends of someone who's dyslexic can support them.

Books and websites about dyslexia are listed on pages 60-61, and the glossary on page 62 explains the more technical words used in the book.

In this book, when we look, for example, at how a dyslexic student is assessed, the student is described as male ('he'). This is not because more boys than girls are dyslexic. What is true, however, is that more boy students are identified as being dyslexic than girl students. Chapter 1 looks at the reasons for this.
Therefore, we have chosen to use 'he', 'his' and 'him'; but remember: whatever is being said would apply equally to girls and women.

A patient helper
A calm, patient friend is a great support for someone struggling with a task such as filling in a form.

1 The dyslexic brain
What makes someone dyslexic?

There are many reasons why some people find it difficult to read and write. It could be because the person is not very bright and has a low intellectual ability. Or perhaps they have undergone emotional trauma in their early life – for example, a death or family problem – and this is 'blocking' their ability to learn. Social or health reasons might have prevented them from going to school, or they may have a physical disability, such as a hearing or visual impairment. However, between one in eight and one in ten of the population finds it more difficult than other people to learn to read and write and there appears to be *no* reason for their difficulty.

These people are of 'normal' intelligence, which means that they are somewhere in the top 95 per cent of the population in terms of their ability to understand and work things out. They have had adequate schooling, and there have been no major emotional or physical problems. And yet they still cannot grasp the idea of letters and words. When the reasons are investigated, it is often discovered that these people are dyslexic. However, it's important to remember that someone can be dyslexic and also have one or more of the other difficulties that have been mentioned.

Some people think that dyslexia is just 'a modern trend' but, in fact, it has been around for hundreds of years. Scholars have studied the writings of Leonardo da Vinci, one of the greatest artists and scientists of all time, who lived in Italy over 500 years ago, and believe that he was

Hidden mystery
In the past, scientists learned about the anatomy of the brain, but understood little about how the brain works.

8

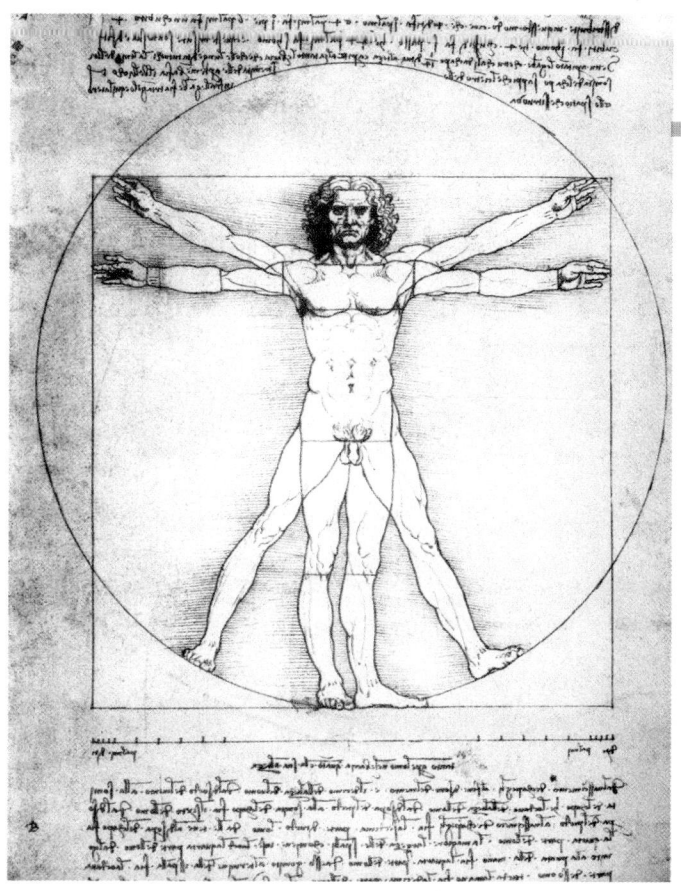

Leonardo da Vinci

This is a famous drawing by the great Renaissance artist Leonardo da Vinci. Artists of the Renaissance period studied nature and science in order to represent the world realistically in their work. Scholars who have studied Leonardo's writing have identified features that suggest he was dyslexic, including 'mirror writing', or writing back to front.

probably dyslexic. However, dyslexia was only brought to light as a condition when, in November 1896, Morgan Pringle, MD, a doctor from Sussex, England, wrote an article in the *British Medical Journal* about a 14-year-old boy called Percy.

The dyslexic brain

At the time Dr Pringle wrote his article, there was very little knowledge about how the human brain works. His article referred to 'Congenital Word Blindness' because it was thought that the problem was to do with eyesight. Since then scientists and doctors have learned much more about the brain and which parts of a dyslexic person's brain process information differently from a non-dyslexic person's brain.

'... he can only with difficulty spell out words of one syllable ... The school master who taught him for some years says that he would be the smartest lad in the school if the instructions were entirely oral.'
(Dr Morgan Pringle, British Medical Journal, 7 November 1896)

The human brain has two halves, or hemispheres, which are linked by a bridge called the *corpus callosum*. In a right-handed person, the left hemisphere is slightly bigger and is dominant.

The two sides of the brain are responsible for processing, or analysing, different things, as the table below shows. For some left-handed people, the right hemisphere is dominant, and so, in their case, the columns in the table would be reversed.

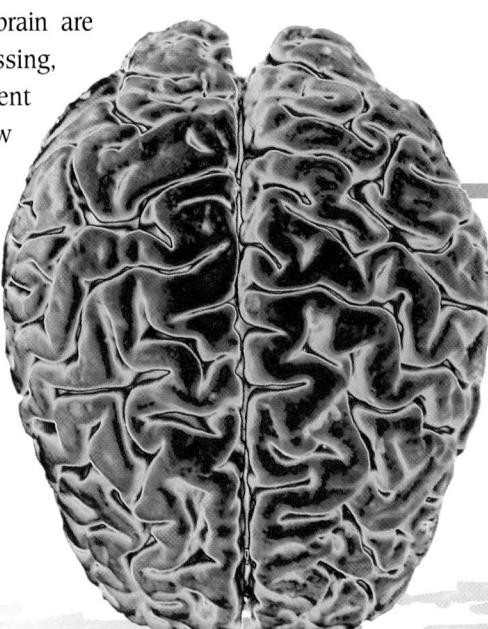

Hemispheres
The two halves of the brain can be seen in this false-coloured brain scan.

Left hemisphere specialization:

- Writing
- Symbols
- Language
- Reading
- Sequences
- Directions
- Logic or reasoning ability
- Structured thinking

Right hemisphere specialization:

- Creativity
- Singing and music
- Spatial relationships – working out where things should go or how things fit together in a given space
- Artistic expression
- Visualization – being able to picture things in your mind
- Feelings and emotions
- Touch
- Intuition or 'gut feelings'
- Fantasy and imagination

What normally happens when we see or hear something is that a message is passed along nerves to the brain. It's like sending the information along wires, into a computer, which remembers and makes sense of the information and then works out what to do about it. This is called **processing**. It usually takes a fraction of a second and we don't even know it's happening. In the case of reading and writing, a non-dyslexic person who has been taught adequately might hear the sound /b/. The message would go into their brain where it would be processed and they would know, almost instantly, to write the letter b. The same would be true the other way round; if they saw the letter b written down, the information would be processed very quickly and they would say the sound /b/ without having to think about it.

For some people though, it isn't that simple. It's as though the wiring is crossed. They will hear the sound /b/ but the message goes to a different part of their brain. They can't always remember what they have heard and the part of the brain that the message has gone to can't make sense of it. They might then write d or p instead of b. When the difficulty is a 'crossed-wires' or processing difficulty, this is what is known as dyslexia.

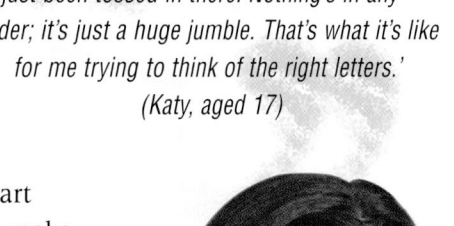

'Imagine trying to find something in a room when everything's just been tossed in there. Nothing's in any order; it's just a huge jumble. That's what it's like for me trying to think of the right letters.'
(Katy, aged 17)

For most dyslexic people the biggest difficulty comes with the processing of sounds. This is called **auditory processing**. For example, a dyslexic person might interpret /g/ as /k/, /m/ as /n/ or /t/ as /d/. It doesn't mean that the person is hearing-impaired; the problem is with the processing of sounds in the brain. Sometimes sounds get in the wrong order and sometimes they're missed out altogether. This often happens with long words and someone who is dyslexic might have difficulty just *saying* words that have three or four syllables, let alone writing them down or reading them. This is because their brain hasn't processed all the parts of the words.

Some dyslexic people have **visual processing** difficulties as well. This means that the information that they *see* also gets directed to a different part of the brain. They might interpret letters as being back to front: p/q for example; or upside down: y/h, w/m and N/Z. Sometimes, parts of the letters have been missed out during the processing; so r/h/n or v/w are confused, for example. Letters can also be in the wrong order. Both auditory and visual processing problems can affect reading, spelling and number work, as we will see in later chapters.

'I had one teacher who just refused to believe me. She kept saying, "Don't tell me you're dyslexic. I've taught someone who was dyslexic and he did such-and-such. You're nothing like him." It was so frustrating.'
(Cindy, aged 16)

Famous people with dyslexia

Thomas Edison *(1857-1931)*
– Inventor of the electric light bulb, microphone and phonograph. He was thought to be a 'dunce' because he couldn't learn the alphabet or his multiplication tables. His writing and spelling were almost unreadable throughout his life.

Some scientists think that the 'crossed wiring' happens when a baby is developing in its mother's womb although, so far, no one is really certain why this happens. It's important to remember that this is a 'developmental' condition. This means that, as the baby is growing, some parts of its brain develop slightly differently from usual. Dyslexia is *not* caused by brain damage, which is when parts of the brain are injured as a result of lack of oxygen or trauma to the head. It's also very important to remember that no two people have the same pattern of difficulties. Every dyslexic person is different in the things they can do well and the things that they find difficult.

The genetic factor

The nucleus of every cell in a human body contains 46 chromosomes arranged in 23 pairs; one of each pair comes from each of our parents. The chromosomes carry the chemical information that determines which features we inherit from our parents. Chromosomes are thin threads that contain DNA (deoxyribonucleic acid). Genes are composed of sections of DNA and are spread out along the chromosomes.

Chromosomes
On the right is a cell nucleus. The thread-like chromosomes are shown in the process of cell division.

It has been thought for a long time that dyslexia runs in families, but until recently scientists have been unable to prove this. Studies have now shown that there is a much higher chance of being dyslexic if there is dyslexia in your family. It is thought that two chromosomes carry the dyslexic genes; chromosome 6 was identified by a team of scientists led by Herbert Lubs from the University of Miami Medical School, and later research, by Dr Shelley D. Smith and scientists from several US universities, indicated that chromosome 15 was also involved. Research is still continuing to find out exactly where on these chromosomes the dyslexic gene is found. The earlier a dyslexic child receives appropriate teaching, the less likely he or she is to fall behind with schoolwork. Therefore it is important to be able to identify which children carry the dyslexic genes as early as possible.

Boys v girls

For many years it was thought that dyslexia affected far more boys than girls. Most specialist dyslexia teachers will tell you that they assess and teach approximately three times as many male students as female ones. However, some scientists now think that it may not be that more boys are born with the dyslexia genes. Researchers are now suggesting that the difference could be to do with the way the female brain adapts, so that other areas of the brain are used to process information.

A team of scientists used MRI (Magnetic Resonance Imaging) scanners to see which areas of the brain are involved with different tasks. Their research showed that, in men, phonological, or sound, processing takes place only in an area of the left hemisphere. In women, this area, together with another area in the right

MRI scanning
The MRI scanning machine produces a 'slice' image of the brain, which appears on the screen in the operator's room.

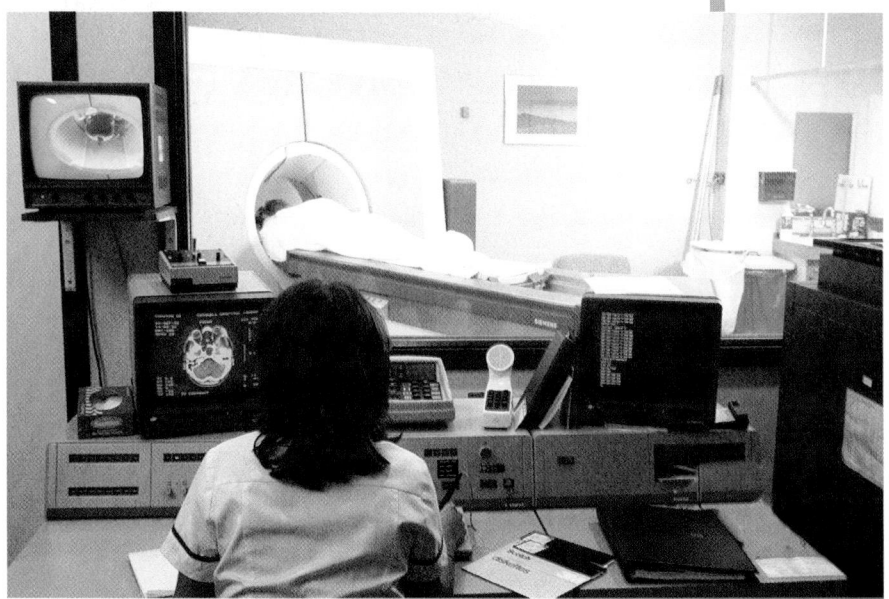

Famous people with dyslexia

Winston Churchill *(1874-1965)*

– British Prime Minister during the Second World War and winner of the Nobel prize for Literature. He hated his school days and had little interest in learning Latin, Greek or maths. His parents were told that he was the worst student in his class.

hemisphere, are both involved. A neurologist called Dr Albert Galaburda has been researching dyslexia for many years. He works at the Beth Israel Deaconess Medical Centre and Harvard Medical School in Boston, USA. He has shown that there are neurological anomalies, or 'different wiring', in certain parts of the brains of dyslexics which are concerned with sound and language. He has imitated this difference in rats and has shown that female rats are more resistant than males to developing this unusual wiring. This may explain why women are less often affected with dyslexia than men. No one knows yet, but more research is unfolding more detail all the time.

Can dyslexia be cured?

The simple answer is no, not at the moment. If a person is born with the neurological anomalies, or different wiring, that make them dyslexic, then they will always be dyslexic. However, the good news is that, with the correct specialist teaching, the vast majority of dyslexic people do make significant improvements in their level of literacy.

Jordan, 15, looks back on his childhood

'By the time I left primary school I wasn't doing much school work at all. The teacher used to sit me at the back of the class to play on the computer. I could hardly read or write. I don't think he knew what to do with me.

When I went to high school, I was a bit of a loner. There was a gang of kids who used to wait for me outside. They'd follow me, calling me names. And then things started to get physical – pushing and tripping up, stuff like that. I got quite depressed and, in the end, I started skipping school. There was an industrial estate near my house and I'd hang around there till it was time to go home. One of the workshops was a motorbike repair centre. I got talking to some of the guys there and I used to watch them.

Of course, Mum and Dad went mad when they found out that I'd been bunking off. But then it all came out about the bullying. I had to see a psychologist and then everyone realized that I wasn't lazy and I wasn't stupid – I'm dyslexic. It felt so good to know that.

I go to a different school now. Part of me thinks it's not fair that it was me who had to leave and not the bullies, but in a way it's been good to make a new start. Mum and Dad have bought me my own Motorcross bike and I go to meetings with it. I can strip down an engine and put it back together, no problems! Even the adults sometimes come to me for advice. It's made a big difference to me, finding something I'm good at.'

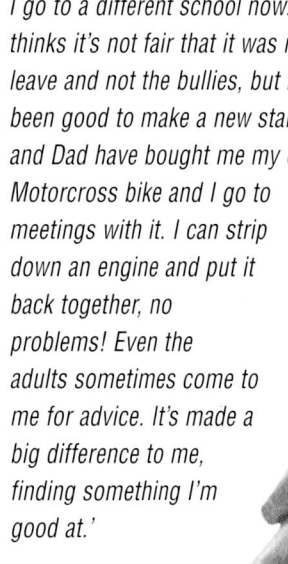

CHAPTER 1

Are there any advantages to being dyslexic?

There are many dyslexic people who believe that their condition gives them an advantage over non-dyslexic people. The same cross-wiring that makes it difficult for their brains to carry out the, normally, left-hemisphere skills, such as reading or putting things in sequence, means that they are better at some of the right-hemisphere skills than people whose brains have been wired in the more usual way. Although, as yet, there is no scientific evidence to prove that this is the case, many dyslexic people believe that they have an enhanced ability in areas such as creativity, artistic expression, imagination and spatial awareness. Spatial awareness is the ability to understand where things go in relation to each other, in both two- and three-dimensional shapes, and many dyslexics find that they have a talent in this area. Good spatial ability is important for many kinds of jobs. Builders, architects, designers, dancers, mechanics, photographers and hairdressers all need this ability.

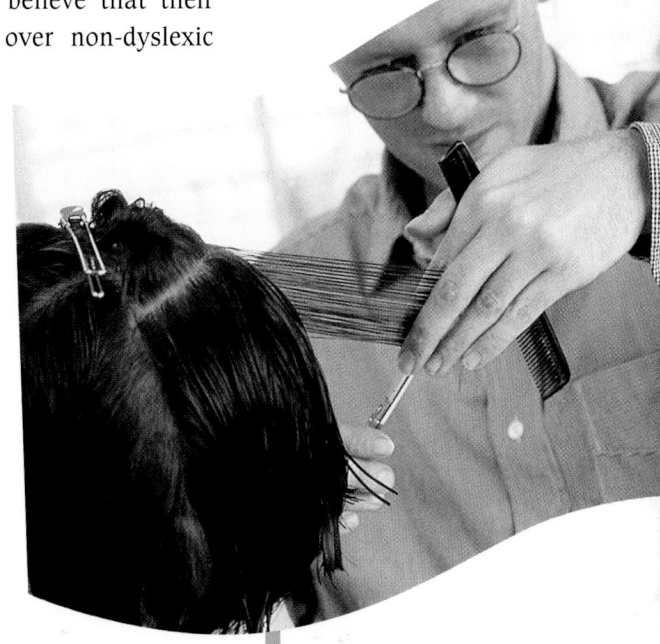

Creating a shape
A hairdresser needs spatial ability for cutting and shaping hair and creating new styles.

Creative thinkers

Many dyslexics find that they excel in what's known as 'lateral thinking'. That means the ability to look at situations from an unusual angle. Again, many dyslexic people believe that they have an advantage over non-dyslexic people in this area because of the way their brains work. Most people, when faced with a challenge, will look at it in small parts and tackle each part individually. This is known as 'bottom-up' thinking. Dyslexic people often have the ability to see situations as a whole and come up with unusual or novel solutions. This is known as 'top-down' thinking.

'I see things differently. Problem-solving is the easy part – it's trying to explain how I got to the answer that's the difficult bit.' (Karen, engineering student)

2 Diagnosing dyslexia
When and how to get assessed

There are several signs that suggest that someone could be dyslexic, and some of them can be recognized from an early age. Some indications are 'persistent'. These are things that are acceptable in young children but don't go away as the person grows up. Examples include muddling right and left, or getting letters such as b and d the wrong way round. Most young children make these mistakes but, as they develop, they usually stop doing so by about the age of seven. In someone who is dyslexic, signs like that might persist throughout their life.

A lifelong struggle
One sign of dyslexia is writing letters like b, d and p the wrong way round. The person will probably have trouble with this all their life.

The signs

In a pre-school child

- Has difficulty matching words that rhyme.
- Has difficulty with putting objects in a sequence, such as coloured beads.
- Has a shorter than average attention span.
- May have been later than normal learning to talk.
- Mixes up words such as 'up' and 'down', or 'in' and 'out'.
- Jumbles up letters in words such as 'par cark' for 'car park'.
- May find it harder than other children to skip, hop, balance, kick a ball.
- Has difficulty dressing himself.
- Finds it hard to clap in time to a rhythm.

The signs

In a primary school child

- Has difficulty learning to read and spell.
- Writes letters and/or numbers the wrong way round.
- Finds it difficult to remember sequences such as the alphabet, days of the week, months of the year, multiplication tables.
- Needs to use his fingers to work out simple calculations.
- Takes longer than others to do written work.
- Leaves out letters or jumbles up the order of letters when reading and writing; was/saw, on/no, etc.
- Confuses left and right.
- Has difficulty tying shoe laces, fastening buttons, tying a tie.
- Seems brighter than his school work suggests.

Literacy
Most children learn the basics of reading and writing in primary school.

Twenty questions

If you are aged 12 years or older, ask yourself the following questions. Do you ...

1. get confused over left and right?
2. make mistakes when you read aloud?
3. take longer than other people to read a page of a book or an article in a newspaper?
4. find it difficult to understand or remember what you've just read?
5. find it difficult to read long books?
6. forget how to spell words? Get the letters in the wrong order or miss out letters?
7. write untidily and is your writing difficult to read?
8. get confused, or tongue-tied, if you have to explain yourself to strangers or groups of people?
9. find it difficult to say long words, like 'phenomenal'?
10. find it difficult to take down phone messages?
11. need to have instructions repeated because you can't remember them?
12. get confused when doing sums in your head?

13. get numbers muddled up? 14 and 41 for example.

14. find it difficult to learn and remember your multiplication tables?

15. find it hard to remember the months of the year in the right order?

16. mix up times or dates and sometimes miss appointments?

17. get confused with timetables?

18. get bus numbers or price tickets mixed up?

19. get confused when saying or writing the alphabet?

20. find it hard to read maps and find your way around a strange place?

Most people will have answered 'Yes' to one or two of these 20 questions. That's completely normal. However, if you are in your teens, or older, and you answered 'Yes' to more than nine of the questions, it is definitely worth investigating the reason. Remember, this is *not* a checklist that can tell you whether someone is or isn't dyslexic. It is simply the first step to getting the right help if you are having difficulties.

'I saw a dress for £12. I looked in my purse and I had just enough money. I queued for ages but, when I got to the check-out, the price came up as £21. I had to go and put the dress back. I felt a complete idiot.'
(Jan, aged 17)

What should you do next?

It's important to have a proper assessment. Some people will say, 'I don't want to be labelled as dyslexic.' But having an assessment has two main advantages which can make an enormous difference to a person who may be struggling with many of the areas on the list and not understand why.

⬤ It identifies the person's strengths and weaknesses so that they can be helped to learn more effectively.

⬤ It offers the person an explanation as to why they are finding some things more difficult than other people. This then helps their family, friends, teachers and employers to understand their difficulties.

The earlier a person is able to get suitable teaching, the less likely they are to fall behind with their reading and writing – but it's never too late to get help.

The assessment process

An educational assessment to diagnose a student's difficulties can be carried out either by an educational psychologist or by a teacher who has been specially trained as an assessor. An educational psychologist is usually someone who has qualified as a chartered psychologist and so they will be able to offer a wider overview of any difficulties that do not fit the dyslexic pattern or 'profile'.

An assessment
A chat with the assessor is followed by several kinds of tests.

Background information

This is an important part of the assessment and usually takes the form of a general chat with the student and his parent or guardian. The assessor finds out about any factors that could have affected the student's ability to learn, such as poor schooling, hearing loss or sight problems, or emotional trauma.

Underlying ability

An educational psychologist normally gives the student some tests, to obtain an IQ (intelligence quotient) score.

This gives an indication of the student's intellectual ability and of what he could reasonably be expected to achieve educationally. A teacher assessor can give a general idea of the student's underlying ability, but would not go into as much depth or offer such an accurate estimate of the student's level of intelligence.

Attainment

The next part of the assessment includes some tests that look at literacy (reading and writing) and, possibly, numeracy (maths). The literacy tests show both how the student reads and spells individual words, and also how he reads and writes continuously. This is because sometimes people can cope with doing one task at a time, such as reading or spelling single words, but, when they have to do lots of things together, there is too much for them to process all at once. Continuous reading or writing involves: working out the letters in each word; remembering the meanings of the words; putting them all together to make sense of the whole passage; and paying attention to punctuation.

Testing reading
The assessor will listen to the way the student reads a piece of continuous text, and will be able to analyse the particular difficulties he has.

Most of the tests carried out in an assessment have been researched using many people of different ages and from many different countries. Tables of scores have been worked out so that the assessor can compare the score of the student who is being assessed against those of other people of the same age and from the same background. These are called 'norms' or 'standardized scores'.

If the assessor sees that the student's score for the intelligence tests was average for his age, but that his reading and spelling scores were well below average, then it is obvious that the student is under-achieving. However, this does not necessarily mean that he is dyslexic.

Performance

This part of the assessment is very important and consists of tests that show the assessor how the student remembers and processes information. They are designed more like puzzles than tests. For example, the student is asked to find the odd one out, or to match up sounds or pictures. He may have to listen to a series of sounds or words and choose ones that match, or he may be asked to remember sequences of numbers or pictures. The assessor also times some of the tests, to see how quickly the student processes information.

'I was really scared. I thought it was going to be like an exam or something and I was going to fail. But it wasn't. I was tired at the end but it was quite good fun really.'
(Luke, aged 11)

The results

Most assessors analyse any reading and spelling mistakes and can work out how the student came to give their response. This is an important part of the assessment. The assessor can also see from the performance tests how well the student processes auditory (heard) information and visual (seen) information, and how strong his memory is.

Performance test
In this test, the student is asked to look at each group of three items and pick the two whose names rhyme.

The assessor then considers the notes he or she has made during the assessment, about how the student was behaving. Did he wriggle about and lose concentration? Did he work out the answers aloud, rather than in his head? Did he ask for questions to be repeated several times? This is because some of the signs of dyslexia are also indications of other difficulties. The assessor needs to build up a picture of the whole person; his background, his intellect, how he processes information and how he behaves in a learning environment. It's like building a jigsaw puzzle and only when this whole puzzle is completed can the assessor make a diagnosis.

Teacher assessor

Melanie is a teacher who took special training in assessing and helping children with literacy problems.

Melanie and Billy

Melanie is a teacher assessor. She talks about one of her clients.

'Billy was 13 when I saw him and by that time he'd been excluded from school several times. He was angry, frustrated and said he didn't care if he was thrown out of school. Billy's dad had read a newspaper article about dyslexia and thought that Billy fitted many of the criteria.

Billy was quite grumpy at the beginning but, as the assessment progressed, he settled down and even seemed to be enjoying himself. By the end, I could see that Billy was a bright boy, easily within the average intelligence band, and he had a very good visual memory. But he had great difficulty recognizing sounds within words, as well as remembering things that were said to him, and his reading and spelling were equivalent to those of a 7-year-old. It was clear that Billy was dyslexic.

Since then Billy has had special lessons. His reading has improved by over 2 years and his spelling by 18 months. So far he hasn't been excluded.'

Working to the strengths

If an assessment shows that a student has a poor auditory memory (remembering things that he has heard), then it is obvious that he will not do very well in a classroom where the teacher does a lot of talking and gives notes using dictation. Likewise, if he is found to have poor visual skills, then there is little point in him being told to 'Look at it and remember.'

'My mum used to give me a shopping list, but I couldn't read it and I couldn't remember the list. She'd go mad when I never bought the right things. Now she understands and we do the list together. I draw pictures and take old labels with me. It works much better.' (Carla, aged 14)

After an assessment, the assessor usually prepares a report which explains the results of the tests. Part of this report will normally be a detailed programme of work designed specifically for the student tested. In an ideal world, the student, his family, teachers, friends and colleagues will all work together so that information is presented in a way that he can understand.

It's important to remember that everyone is different, and what works for one person may not work for another. The best way for anyone to learn is to use their strengths in order to boost their weaker areas. Ways of doing this will be looked at in future chapters.

Famous people with dyslexia

Hans Andersen *(1805-75)*

– Writer of many of our most well-known fairy stories, such as 'The Ugly Duckling'. Recent analysis of his handwriting has shown that he was dyslexic.

3 Reading and writing
Cracking the code

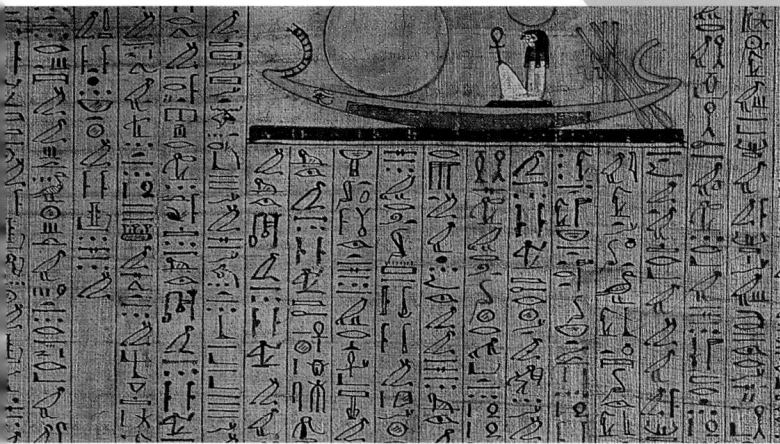

Ancient Egypt
The Ancient Egyptians used picture symbols to represent words.

The history of reading and writing

Ancient civilizations such as the Egyptians began creating written symbols as long ago as 2000 BCE. In those days, the symbols were more like picture representations of words. Then the Ancient Romans and Greeks developed systems of writing down language sound by sound, in much the same way as we do in the Western world today.

For centuries, learning how to read and write was largely restricted to the wealthy people – royalty, religious leaders, politicians and scholars. The vast majority of people never learned how to read and write because ancient societies didn't require it. Skills and trades were passed down from father to son and from mother to daughter, by imitation. Information was circulated by word of mouth. It is only during the last 100 to 150 years that literacy has been made available to almost everyone.

To realize how dependent we have become on written language, just look around you. See how many pieces of writing there are: books, magazines, letters, labels, notices. Next time you walk down the street, notice every poster, billboard, shop or traffic sign that uses written language.

Ancient Greece
The Ancient Greeks developed an alphabet of letters representing different sounds. The writing here gave thanks to the god of healing for the cure of a bad leg.

Kyle helps his mum

Kyle, 13, talks about how his mum's dyslexia affects him too.

'When my mum was at school no one knew much about dyslexia, so she's never been told officially that she's dyslexic, but I'm pretty sure she is. She's really clever, but she can hardly read and write and she gets letters and numbers back to front. She can't remember her alphabet or anything like that, either.

When I was a little kid, she took me to the hospital once and she couldn't find her way about. She kept asking people directions but couldn't remember them and couldn't read the signs. We went round and round the hospital and in the end we were late for my appointment and the doctor went mad. She started crying and so did I.

Dad left us when I was a baby, so ever since I've been at school I've done all the reading and writing stuff for her – reading her letters, putting notes out for the milkman and things like that. I even have to write my own absence notes for school and one day I got a detention because the teacher accused me of forging the letter.'

How we read

Learning to read is a very complicated process. Reading just one single word requires us to:

- move our eyes across the text in the correct direction; in the Western world this is left to right
- take in the visual information from the paper – the shapes of the letters and the order of the letters
- relay this information through the nervous system to the brain
- process, or analyse, the information
- memorize it
- retrieve from our auditory memory the sounds that are associated with the letters
- blend the sounds together in the correct order
- say the word.

How we spell

Spelling is no less complicated and requires us to:

- remember the word we want to write or, if we are taking dictation, hear the word
- relay this information through the nervous system to the brain
- separate out the sounds in the word
- memorize them in the correct order
- retrieve from our auditory memory the letters that are associated with the sounds
- decide which spelling rules might apply
- relay this information through the nervous system to the hand
- direct the hand to form the letters correctly in a left to right direction
- read the word to check that it says what we wanted it to say.

Everyday sight

Our towns are full of billboards, posters and signs of all kinds. We probably do not realize the complex processes involved in reading them.

Code-breaking

Spelling is known as 'encoding' because it's about building up a code of letters that represent sounds. The reverse process, of breaking down and working out a word that we read, is called 'decoding'. The decoding and encoding processes might not be too difficult if each sound had just one letter that was used to represent it, but, in English, some letters are associated with more than one sound.

When we're reading, the sound that we say when we see a letter depends on the other letters around it. For example, the vowels (a, e, i, o and u) all have two sounds. One is short and clipped, such as short /a/ for 'apple'. The other is longer and is the long sound which is also the name of the vowel, such as /A/ for acorn.

Whether we say a vowel as a short sound or a long sound depends on how many consonants come after it. Consonants are all the letters that are not vowels, such as b, c, d, f, etc. If there's only one consonant after a vowel, then we usually say the vowel as a long sound. If there is more than one consonant after a vowel, then it's usually said as the short sound.

Other letter sounds can be even more confusing; c is said /k/, as in 'cat'; but if the next letter is i, e, or y, then the c is said /s/, as in 'city'. And if the letter that comes after c is h, then we put the two letters together and say one sound /ch/, as in 'chips'. And just to complicate things a bit more, if the ch is followed by r, or if it comes in the middle of a word, then we ignore the h and go back to saying the c as /k/ – for example, in 'Christmas' or 'school'.

Work it out!

Can you work out what the word ghoti says?

The answer is fish.
   gh = /f/, as in cough,
   o = /i/ as in women
   and ti = /sh/ as in station.

Building up a sight vocabulary

Most people, though, don't even have to think about all those different things when they're reading and writing. For the majority of people, learning to read and spell is a relatively painless process. They develop an understanding of sounds and words before they start school and quickly pick up the idea of the written word. Once they can decode and encode the simple words, such as 'cat', they can create a memory-store of information on which they can draw as the words become longer and more complicated. This is known as their 'sight vocabulary'.

'I read the words on the side of a van and said, "Shoplifters? That's a bit blatant isn't it? How come they don't get arrested?" My friends laughed at me because the van actually said, "Shopfitters".'
(Alan, aged 18)

Cracking up under the code?

For someone who is dyslexic, however, all sorts of problems may arise. If they have difficulty with identifying the sounds in spoken language, it's likely that matching up the symbols with the sounds would cause the first major stumbling block. 'Cat' may be read as 'c-o-d' or even 'c-ate', because they can't remember which sounds go with the letters a and t. If their difficulties are with the blending of sounds, they may know that the sounds are c-a-t but not be able to blend them together to make a fluent word.

Add to that, possible visual processing difficulties, and they may read the word as 'act' or 'tac'. Also, many dyslexic people have a poor short-term memory, and so they don't build up the memory bank of sight words on which most people rely for fluent reading.

Similar problems would apply to spelling. A student with weak auditory processing might write the word 'cat' as 'ct' or 'ced', because the vowel sound has not been processed correctly and the /t/ and /d/ sounds have become confused. Weak visual processing might mean that the t has been inverted so that it looks like 'caf'. Alternatively, the student might have recognized the /k/ sound but not been able to remember whether it was k or c. Hence he could, quite realistically, write 'kof', thinking that he had written 'cat'.

These examples are using one of the simplest three-sound words there is, and yet some extremely bright people have difficulty even at this level. Imagine, then, the problems with complex, polysyllabic words (words with several syllables) such as 'phenomenally' or 'hierarchical'!

Continuous reading and writing

The problems dyslexic people have are often multiplied when they are faced with reading a passage of a book or an article in a newspaper, or writing a letter or essay.

Reading a piece of continuous writing means that we have to remember all the previous words we have read in the passage, in order to make sense of the whole piece. We also need to understand the punctuation – all those full stops, commas, speech marks, colons, semi-colons, question marks and exclamation marks, which help us to read with meaning.

'People don't understand because it seems as if I can read fluently. But reading has always been an effort. I'd never read a whole book until I was in my 20s and I often have to read a paragraph up to five times for it to make sense.'
(Polly, a teacher)

A good read?
When words are linked in passages of text, the problems can be magnified for people with dyslexia.

Likewise, when we are writing, we need to remember what we've already written, as well as think ahead to what we want to write so that it all makes sense.

For someone with dyslexia, the same types of problems arise with words within sentences as with letters in individual words. Words get jumbled up and missed out, and some words are worked out as saying something different from what they actually say.

Even people who are mildly dyslexic, and can decode or encode individual words accurately, often find reading a whole book or writing an essay quite overwhelming.

What can be done?

Conventional teaching methods rely heavily on the students being able to process the information they are given quickly and accurately and then remember it. Information is taken in using the senses, mainly sight and hearing. But when there is a difficulty with the processing of information received through either or both of these senses, then it's unlikely that the teaching will be very effective. For this reason, specialist dyslexia teaching is most effective when it is what's known as structured multisensory teaching.

'One teacher threw my book in the bin. I could write the same word fifty times and I still wouldn't be able to spell it. A spellcheck helps but even then, I don't always know which word to choose if it offers me more than one alternative.'
(Echo Freer, author)

CHAPTER 3

What is structured multisensory teaching?

Structured means built up in a logical progression and multisensory means using many senses.

Everyone, whether dyslexic or not, remembers things much better when they have experienced them for themselves. If we simply listen to something, we forget most of it. If we see something, we remember it a bit more. But when we are actively involved in doing something, we are far more likely to understand and remember it. Therefore, multisensory teaching does just that; it actively involves the student in learning about sounds and the symbols that represent them, using many senses. Wooden or plastic letters are used so that the student *hears* the sound, *says* the sound and can *see* and *feel* the letter that is used to represent it. Words are built up using the wooden or plastic letters so that the student can experience creating words physically as he hears and repeats the sounds.

Sometimes, with younger children, multisensory teaching is done in groups, but this type of teaching is more effective if it's done one-to-one. This is because everyone learns differently and at different speeds and also, older students, particularly those who are still in school, are often embarrassed about using what can be seen as 'childish' methods.

Learning by feel
This boy is being taught the alphabet using capital letters. His teacher also has a set of lower-case wooden letters for teaching him spellings.

'When I started lessons I thought, there's no way I'm doing that baby stuff! But after a few weeks I could see that it was working. People had tried to teach me to read for years, but using the wooden letters is the only thing that's made any sense to me.'
(Peter, aged 15)

A magic wand?

Multisensory teaching is not a magic wand that produces instant results. If a student is bright and begins specialist teaching when he is young, up to about 7 years of age, then the improvement can be, and often is, dramatic. However, the more normal pattern is one of hard work and gradual improvement, sometimes over many years. The older a person is before he has access to specialist tuition, the harder it is likely to be for him. The good news is that the majority of dyslexic people, of whatever age, can and do make improvements in their level of literacy if they are taught in the appropriate way.

Helping with reading

Here are some tried and tested ideas for helping a dyslexic friend or relation with reading:

- *Always ask the person what support they want and how they want you to be. The reader must always be the one in charge.*
- *If the person is reading fluently and keeping the general idea of the piece, don't correct every mistake.*
- *If he has made a mistake which alters the meaning, wait until he's finished the sentence and then suggest that he goes back and checks the word again.*
- *If he is struggling with a word, encourage him to work from left to right, sounding out the letters and blending them into syllables and words.*
- *Always use sounds rather than letter names. For example, say, k-a-t and blend it to say 'cat'. Saying C A T, which blends as 'seeaytee', won't be much help!*
- *If he can't work out a word, don't let him struggle; supply it for him quickly and move on.*
- *It sometimes helps to read the first sentence or paragraph aloud for him so that he can get the general idea and tone of the book or article.*
- *Suggest that he listens to set books on tape or watches them on video first so that he has a rough idea of the story and characters before he starts reading.*

Helping with spelling

These are tried and tested ways for helping someone with spelling:

- *Always break words down into manageable parts:*
    - *Say the word as a whole.*
    - *Then say it as separate syllables.*
    - *Take the first syllable and say the sounds individually. (Never say the letter names.)*
    - *Blend the sounds together and repeat that syllable.*
    - *Encourage him to say the sounds as he is writing them.*
- *The dyslexic person should always be the one to check what he has written.*
- *Don't point out every spelling mistake in a piece of writing. Instead, point out any patterns of spelling mistakes.*
- *Ask teachers not to mark down work because of poor spelling, handwriting or punctuation.*
- *Always be positive and encouraging.*

Helping a friend

Friends can be a great help if they understand each other's strengths and weaknesses.

Ways of learning and remembering

VISUAL	AUDITORY	KINESTHETIC
You can learn by looking at: - Pictures - Videos and television - Diagrams - Computers - Colour-coding - Visualizations in your 'mind's eye' - Spidergrams	You can learn by listening to: - Lectures and talks - Audio tapes and radio - Dictation	You can learn by: - Using physical objects such as concept cards or jigsaws - Inventing card games or board games to help learning become fun - Playing interactive computer games or learning programs - Making spidergrams - Active learning – doing things to see if they work - Going on visits or field trips - Using touch, feel and movement as much as possible - Seeing, saying, hearing and doing all at once

Use the ways of learning and remembering that best suit your skills. If your visual and auditory skills are weak, use kinesthetic methods.

If someone has a weak auditory memory, it is unlikely he will be able to learn something simply by listening and repeating it. He will probably need to use visual and kinesthetic ways of remembering as well. Kinesthetic means doing something physically, so that we remember the feel of something and the actions we did. Just as learning to read and write is more effective if multisensory methods are used, so the dyslexic person will benefit from using multisensory means to learn other skills.

Computer game

Playing an interactive computer game helps ideas to stick in your memory.

Albert Einstein *(1879-1955)*

– One of the greatest scientists of all time. He developed the Theory of Relativity, but he did not learn to read until he was nine and failed his first entrance exam to college.

Mathematics and numbers

Not everyone who is dyslexic has difficulty with maths: take Albert Einstein, for example. And not everyone who has difficulty with maths is dyslexic. But research has shown that the proportion of dyslexic people who struggle with arithmetic is significantly higher than the proportion of non-dyslexic people who have difficulty with numbers. Estimates suggest that between 40 and 70 per cent of people who are dyslexic also have difficulty with arithmetic.

Some of the ways maths may be difficult for someone who is dyslexic

- *Written instructions may be misread; words or numbers may be missed out or read the wrong way round.*
- *Numbers may be read or written back to front or even upside down:*
  42 for 24,   6 for 9,   5 for 2,   L for 7, etc.
- *Visual processing difficulties can often lead to signs being misread:*
  + for x   + for –,   – for ÷, etc.
  (This can also happen when using calculators.)
- *Sequencing difficulties can cause problems with counting and multiplication tables.*
- *Poor short-term memory can cause problems when doing mental arithmetic; a dyslexic person may use his fingers when trying to work out sums in his head.*
- *Place value can cause problems for some people who may have visual difficulties. They often put the numbers in the wrong columns.*
- *Algebraic and geometric symbols can also cause problems.*

However, it's also true that the same areas in which some dyslexic people believe that they often excel, such as spatial awareness and lateral thinking, can also benefit them in maths. Someone who has good spatial awareness will probably find that they do well with geometry and trigonometry. Someone who is able to think laterally is likely to do well with investigations and problem-solving exercises.

Concept cards

These examples of concept cards show ways of expressing one; and ways of expressing one quarter. A different colour is used for each set of cards. This helps the student to link the ideas on the cards.

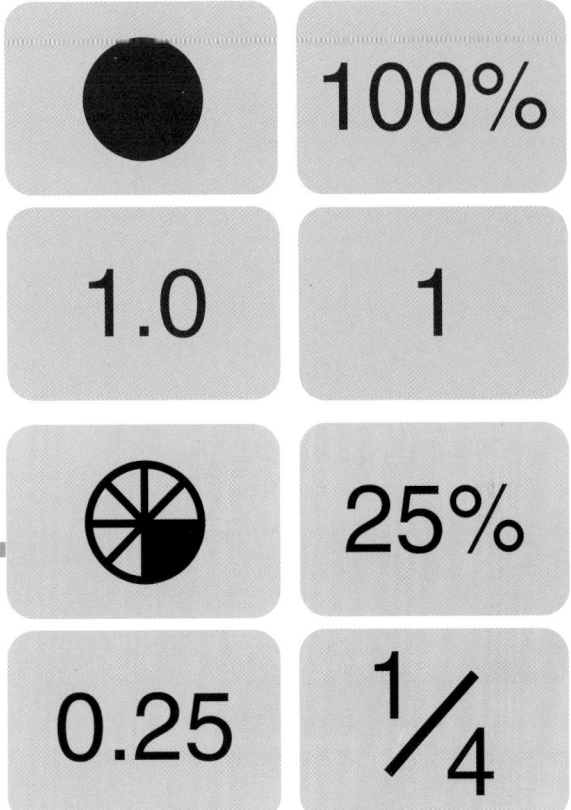

Helping with maths

These are some useful strategies for helping a dyslexic person with maths:

- *Make maths understandable: use physical things such as beads and blocks so that the person can grasp the concept of numbers.*
- *Use concept cards – these are cards which link ideas. For example, number bonds: 9 = 8 + 1, 6 + 3, 4 + 5, 3 x 3, etc.*
- *Once a person has the ability to estimate fairly accurately, don't stop them using a calculator. As long as they have the ability to realize when the answer looks wrong, there is little point in letting them struggle.*
- *Fractions and decimals can be explained by using real food – cakes, chocolate bars, apples, etc.*
- *Never deter someone from using their own individual way of working out sums – as long as it works!*

Dyscalculia

Some people who have no difficulty with understanding words, sounds and letters, do have problems with maths. This condition is known as **dyscalculia**. Not much is known about dyscalculia, but it is thought to affect the way people understand simple numbers and mathematical concepts in the same way that dyslexia affects the way some people understand sounds and letters. Dyscalculia is thought to affect fewer people than dyslexia, but research is continuing in this area.

Music v musical notation?

It is often said that people who are dyslexic find music difficult. Well, that's not strictly true. Music is an abstract art form and involves individual interpretation, and so the same right–hemisphere specialization applies to music as to other creative skills. This means that some dyslexic people find that they excel in both musical appreciation and musical creativity.

Joel's musical talent

Joel, now 18, was diagnosed as being dyslexic when he was seven.

'Music's always been important to me. I got a guitar when I was 12 but, when I started to have lessons, it was really difficult. In the end I asked my teacher to stop trying to teach me from the book and teach me by ear. It worked and I got so good that I used to play lead guitar in two bands. I'm studying Music Technology at college now and I compose my own music on computer. I can't begin to describe how satisfying it is to hear something that I've created.'

What many dyslexic people do often have problems with, however, is musical notation – the way in which music is written down using symbols. The mechanics of working out, remembering, sequencing and applying words and names to marks and symbols is often extremely difficult for people who have dyslexic difficulties. This is particularly so when the symbols are all of the same shape – and when that shape is similar to two of the letters that cause problems in reading and spelling: d and p.

'Every time I look at a piece of manuscript paper it's like reading some sort of alien language written in ds and ps. A fuse in my mind blows. It's like trying to find a picture in one of those magic eye things.' (Jacob, aged 11)

Here are some points about musical notation, which make it especially difficult for dyslexic musicians:

- To read the music, the musician's eyes have to move not only from left to right but also up and down at the same time.
- The same-shaped symbol is used in different places on the staves to represent the pitch of a note.
- Only small differences indicate how long a note should be held.
- There are likely to be sequencing difficulties with remembering which note is on which stave.
- Scales and key signatures are also likely to be affected by sequencing difficulties – remembering which notes are sharp or flat in a particular key.
- Many musical terms are written in Italian, which can be an extra difficulty for someone who has problems with reading in their own native language.

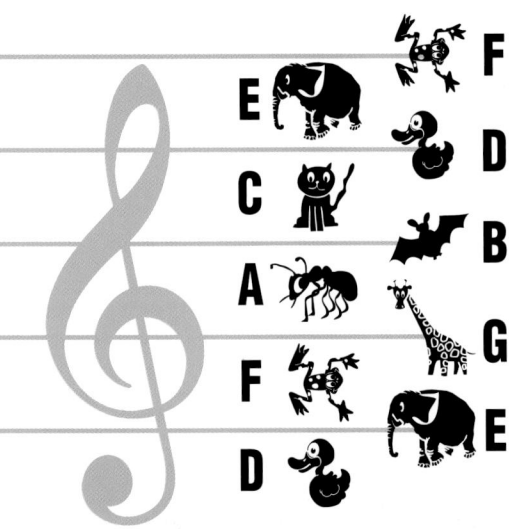

Picture clues

Using picture clues helps to jog your memory as to where the musical notes are, whether you are learning about written music (above) or about the keys on a keyboard. Some people visualize the pictures while others use stickers. The duck would remind you which note is D.

Some strategies that have helped musicians

- *Using picture clues to remember which note is on which stave. It helps if the pictures are linked, such as food, or animals; for example, e = elephant, g = goat, b = bird, d = dog, f = fish.*
- *Using mnemonics such as 'Every Good Boy Deserves Fun' – another way to remember which note is on which stave: EGBDF.*
- *Using cream or off-white paper to write music, as this reduces glare and helps with visual processing.*

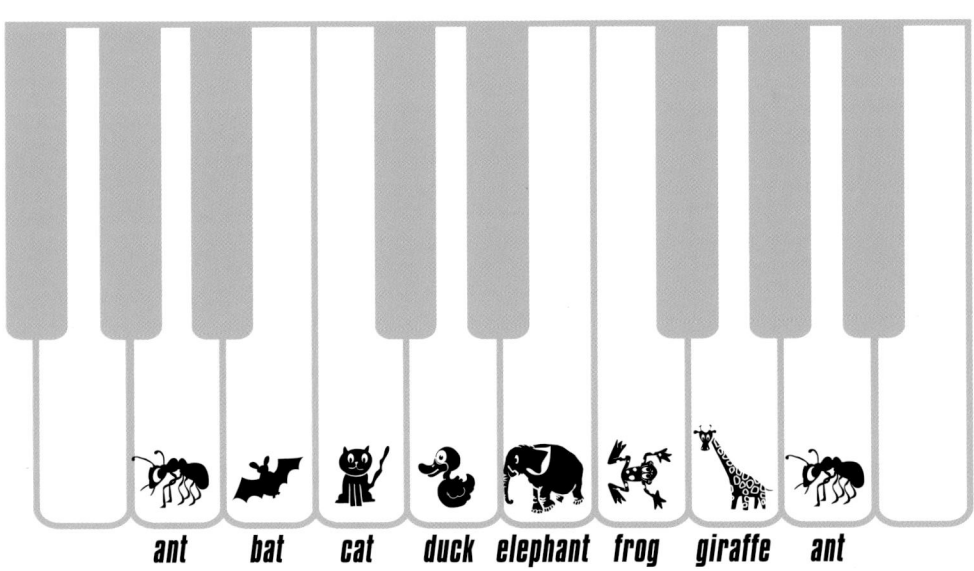

ant bat cat duck elephant frog giraffe ant

Time trouble

There are two main areas of difficulty around time. Firstly, some dyslexic people have no understanding of the passage of time. If someone finds it difficult to remember things in order, then the sequence of events and the length of time between events are often muddled. Some dyslexic people cannot differentiate between five minutes, ten minutes and half an hour. They will not be able to tell you whether something happened two days ago or five days ago, last week or last month or last year. Forward planning becomes difficult because there is nothing concrete for them to hang phrases onto, like 'tomorrow', 'next week', 'in three months', 'next year'.

Max at work

Max is a graphic designer.
'People who don't know me think I'm lying because when they ask me a question that starts with, "How long …", my mind goes blank. I usually say something like, "Five years." I haven't got a clue how long five years is and it's got me into all sorts of trouble. One guy said, "How long have you worked here?" I said, "Five years." And then he pointed out that I'd have been at school five years ago.

The other thing is, if my train's delayed by 20 minutes, I don't know what that means. Have I got time to buy a coffee? Will it be quicker to walk, or what? I can work out what the time is on my watch so, if I'm told I've got an hour for lunch, I know when to be back. But I don't have any idea what I can do in that time, so I often get back really early or really late. My friends are cool about it, but I don't want everyone to know about my dyslexia because not everyone understands, so I don't tell many people.'

The second difficulty with time can come with the technical side of time-telling. If the dyslexic person has difficulties with numbers and fractions, it is more than likely that they will have difficulties making links between numbers and time on an analogue clock face. Some of the things which might confuse them would be:

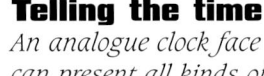

- Why does the number 1 represent 5 minutes?
- How can the number 6 also be 30 minutes and a half-hour?
- Why is the interval between 10 and 11, 5 minutes?
- How can 5 and 7 both represent 25?
- There might also be language difficulties with the terms 'past' and 'to'.

Telling the time
An analogue clock face can present all kinds of problems for someone with dyslexia.

Even using a digital clock doesn't always overcome all the difficulties, because numbers can be reversed. Imagine arriving for your train at 8:52 to find that it left at 8:25. If the digital clock is a twenty-four hour clock, there

Famous people with dyslexia

Woodrow Wilson

(1856-1924)

– President of the USA during the First World War. He did not learn to read until he was eleven and was thought to be 'a dullard' at school.

can be the mental arithmetic difficulties of subtracting 12 to work out the times between 12 noon and 12 midnight.

It is not unusual for dyslexic people to regularly miss appointments or be late. This is not because they can't be bothered, but because of a condition that they cannot help. If you find yourself feeling annoyed because your dyslexic friend is repeatedly late, try to imagine what life must be like for him!

Strategies that have helped some people with time

◉ *Physically marking off certain time periods, days on a calendar, or hours on a timetable.*

◉ *Using a timeline for any given period, be it in historical terms or in the person's own life. Mark off set periods, such as months, years, decades or centuries. Draw pictures or symbols to represent significant events and place them on the timeline.*

Timeline
Drawing pictures helps make sense of the sequence of events.

Laterality

Lateral means 'of the side' and laterality is about which side of a person is dominant, right or left. Most people find that if they're right-handed for writing, then they use their right hand for throwing and their right foot for kicking and their right eye is dominant. That means that it is stronger and takes control over the left eye. They also learn which side is right and which is left by about the age of seven, and this knowledge becomes automatic.

'If I was driving and someone said "Turn right," I would panic. I've put stickers on my windscreen now. There's an apple at one side and a banana at the other, so if someone's directing me, they say, "Take the next turning to the banana." It never fails.' (Ronnie, aged 18)

For someone who's dyslexic, however, there is often 'mixed dominance'. That means that their right side is stronger for some things and their left side for others. For example, they might write and throw with their right hand but kick with their left foot, and their left eye might be dominant. And they often find it difficult to remember which is right and which is left. Ask someone who's dyslexic to stand on their left leg and they often have to think very hard, or use physical means such as doing imaginary writing, before they will know which is their left foot – and even then they may get it wrong!

Southpaw boxer

This boxer is left-handed, but he could have a dominant right eye and foot, making him 'mixed dominance'.

Directions and map-reading

Knowing the directions is another area which is rife with difficulties for someone who's dyslexic. Remembering the terms north, south, east and west is difficult in itself. They are not usually said in the order that they appear on a compass. If someone has poor visual skills, applying the directions to a map can cause additional confusion. For example, if the dyslexic person is travelling south, they may not be able to associate the direction of travel they are physically experiencing with going downwards on the map. They may feel disorientated. They often find it easier to track their movements if they turn the map upside down so that it seems as though they are moving forwards up the map. However, this will mean that the road names are upside down. Repeatedly turning the map the right way up to read it and then back to the direction of travel can lead to the person losing their place. It can be even more awkward if the map is fixed to a wall and it can't be turned round. Finding the way around a new school or college can be a nightmare for some students who are dyslexic – even if there are plans at the corner of every corridor.

Finding the way

A map and a compass are guides to help us find the way, but using them requires particular skills that we don't all have.

W. B. Yeats *(1865-1939)*
– Poet who won the Nobel prize for Literature.
His father got so impatient with him that he
flung the reading book at his head. His
handwriting and spelling were atrocious and he
had difficulty with pronunciation when he tried
to read his own poetry out loud.

Foreign languages

We have already discussed the difficulties of learning to read and write for someone who's dyslexic – and that's in the language they have been speaking since early childhood. Imagine then the difficulties of learning a new language.

- The student has to remember thousands of new words for nouns (names of objects) and verbs (doing words) that he has been using other names for for years.

- Foreign languages often have different spoken sounds in them. These are unfamiliar and so are difficult to process.

- Different languages often have different alphabets. They may be similar to our own alphabet but with some letters slightly altered by accents or umlauts. Some foreign alphabets, such as Russian or Greek, consist of letters that are completely different.

- Different languages often put words in a different order within a sentence. For example, some languages put the verb near the beginning of the sentence whilst others have it at the end.

- Gender – that is whether something is male, female or neutral – and how that is represented can vary from language to language.

Strategies that have helped some people with languages

- Write vocabulary in a different colour for each gender.
- Record words or phrases onto tape and then listen back to them several times. A walkman is suitable for this.
- Create your own jigsaw puzzle cards for sentence structure: write out several sentences, cut them up, then try to reconstruct them correctly.
- Work in twos as much as possible. It makes learning more fun.

We're all different

Not everyone who is dyslexic will have problems with all of the areas covered in this chapter. However the 2 to 4 per cent of the population who are severely dyslexic are likely to experience difficulties with most of the skills that have been discussed. And dyslexia is not something that is obvious to another person. If someone has a wheelchair or a hearing aid, then most people will understand that their ability in some areas may be restricted. They are likely to be treated with a degree of understanding and patience.

This is not always the case with someone who is dyslexic. Their difficulties cannot be seen, but the effects of dyslexic difficulties can be and, unfortunately, often are met with impatience or criticism. The most important word when dealing with someone who is dyslexic is patience. If you feel annoyed or irritated when someone is repeatedly late or gets lost or can't add up, take a second to imagine how frustrating it must be for them.

Learning a language by ear

When you listen to a language and repeat it, you become used to the pronunciation and sentence structure without having to worry about the spelling and writing.

5 The dyslexic student
Techniques for success

Dyslexia in the classroom

As we have seen, the most beneficial thing is to make things multisensory; to learn through doing, feeling, saying, hearing and seeing, all at the same time. However, when someone who is dyslexic is in a classroom with twenty or more students, many of whom do not have difficulties with processing information, it can be tough on both the student and the teacher. Some of the difficulties might be:

- The student may be able to understand the level of work that is being taught but be slower processing the information.
- He may panic and 'blank' when asked a direct question.
- He may find reading text books difficult.
- His copying, both from the board and from a text book, may be inaccurate.
- He may forget instructions such as what equipment to bring.
- He may not be able to process the information quickly enough to take down dictation.
- He may reverse numbers and therefore read, or do work from, the wrong pages.
- He may be embarrassed about his level of work and so appear difficult and disruptive in order to direct attention away from his reading and writing.
- He may use humour for similar reasons, becoming the class clown.

In a classroom situation, it's not always practical or appropriate for a teacher to give the whole group work that is multisensory. But there are things that can be done, which could make lessons easier for everyone.

If you are dyslexic:

- 🌀 *Do talk to your teacher or tutor about your difficulties and what works best for you.*
- 🌀 *If you do not feel confident to approach a teacher, tell a trusted friend what it is you want the teacher to know and ask your friend to come with you. If you forget what you want to say, or get tongue-tied, your friend will be able to support you.*
- 🌀 *Use a Dictaphone to take down details of homework quickly.*
- 🌀 *If you find it hurtful to hear people telling jokes about dyslexia, tell them. Otherwise they'll never know and may carry on doing it.*

Stop the critic
Don't let anyone make upsetting comments about dyslexia.

If you know someone who's dyslexic:

- ⚙ Ask them how you can support them. Don't just presume they want something read to them or written for them.

- ⚙ Always be positive. Ignore any mistakes they might make and praise them when they do things well.

- ⚙ Never make fun of them or put them down – and that doesn't just go for people who are dyslexic either!

Dictating

It is sometimes helpful for a student with dyslexia to dictate their work. The friend taking it down must write exactly what the student says. They should not alter it in any way, even if they think they are helping by improving it.

If you teach someone who's dyslexic:

- ⚙ Ask them what works best for them and listen to their reply.

- ⚙ Be tactful; don't single the student out and make them appear different.

- ⚙ If appropriate, prepare worksheets that will stretch the dyslexic student intellectually but which require less reading and writing.

- ⚙ Accept typed or dictated written work.

Mark, 14, loves learning

'When I started secondary school I was put in the lowest set for most subjects. I was furious. I knew that I was cleverer than everyone else in my tutor group. Then, after about a term, I think some of the teachers realized that I shouldn't really be in the lowest set. I had an assessment and was told that I was dyslexic. It was such a relief. I've been having special lessons ever since. I'm in Year 9 now and I'm in the top set for every subject except Spanish. My reading is still slow but I can work out most words. I still need help with spelling though. I do most of my homework on a PC. I don't know what I want to do when I leave school. I'm definitely going to go to university though. I'd like to do something with computers.'

Spidergrams

Spidergrams, also known as pictograms or mind maps®, are one of the most effective ways for the majority of people to learn, whether they are dyslexic or not.

Most forms of note-taking are linear, which means 'in a line'. In the West, we are taught from an early age to write from left to right, moving down the page, and so one page of our exercise book looks very much like another. It can be difficult when it comes to revising for an exam, because there is nothing to help us remember one page from another, apart from the words. By contrast, looking at a spidergram uses right and left hemispheres of our brain.

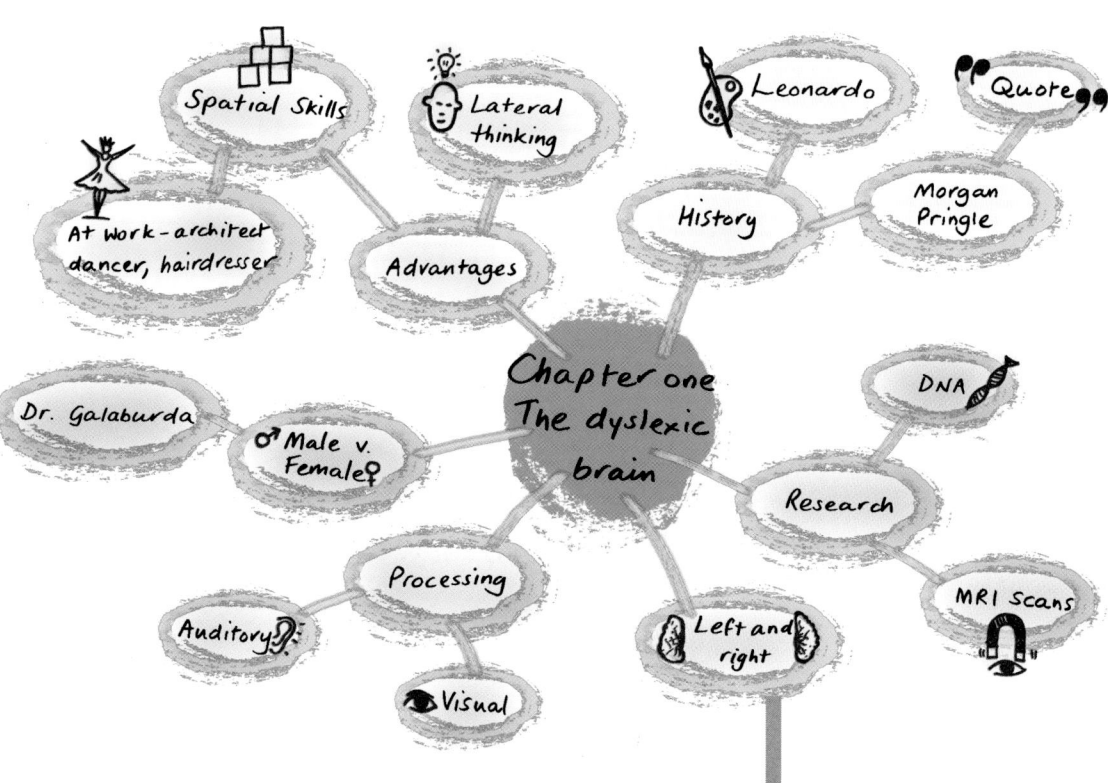

We use the spatial aspect to remember where things are on the spidergram, and colours on it are another element to jog our memories.

Here's how to draw a spidergram:

- Put the central idea or theme in the centre of the page.
- Draw branches out from the centre for each sub-topic.
- Draw each sub-topic in a different colour.
- Smaller branches come off each of the big branches as the sub-topic is expanded.
- Use the same colour for all related information.
- Use drawings, symbols or diagrams to represent facts wherever possible.

Unlike written notes, additional information can easily be added to a spidergram later.

Spidergram

Here's a spidergram used to plan chapter 1 of this book.
You don't have to be Picasso to draw a spidergram! The drawing is for you, not for anyone else. So, as long as you know what a symbol means, that is all that matters.

How computers can help

We are living in an electronic age and computers can offer many advantages as a way of reinforcing lesson material at a student's own pace. Learning keyboarding, or touch-typing, is essential. That means knowing where the keys are without having to look at the keyboard and search for each letter. Some of the advantages of using a computer are:

- Computers are fun and motivating.
- Computers do not criticize, lose their patience or poke fun if you make mistakes.
- The nature of computer software means that programs are structured and easy to follow.
- Programs can be repeated as many times as needed.
- There is now voice-activated software, which can be particularly useful for those whose spelling is very weak.
- Typing means that you do not have to be concerned with the technical side of forming letters.
- Spelling becomes automatic through typing, and writing is faster.

The Thinker

The most famous work by Rodin is a sculpture called 'The Thinker' ('Le Penseur' in French).

Famous people with dyslexia

Auguste Rodin (1840-1917)

– Artist and sculptor. He was once described as 'the worst pupil in the school.' His father said, 'I have an idiot for a son.' At the age of 14, Rodin was enrolled into the 'School for Workers', as he had failed three times to pass the entrance exam to the 'School for Artists'. Today, there are entire museums dedicated to his work in Paris and New York.

Exams

Exams can be a stressful time for most people, but the difficulties that come with being dyslexic are often increased under the pressure of revising and sitting exams. It's worth checking with your teacher and examination board what, if any, special arrangements can be made for dyslexic students.

Getting ready
*Collect everything you will
need to take into the exam.*

Making exams less stressful

Revision

- Make it fun – revise in twos and quiz each other.
- Make it manageable. Set time limits. Stretches of 30 to 40 minutes are ideal, with a 10-minute break between.
- Make it memorable. Use spidergrams and colour.

The exam

- Check that you've got the right date and time.
- Find a way that suits you to remember the equipment you will need.
- Plan your time. Allocate an appropriate amount of time for each question, depending on how many marks it's worth.
- Allow time at the end for checking.
- Plan each question. If you've allowed 20 minutes to answer a question, spend 5 minutes planning, 12 minutes writing and 3 minutes checking.
- Be strict with your time. Don't be tempted to spend a little bit longer on one question because you know a lot about it.
- Try to remain calm. Panic never helped anyone.

It is sometimes possible to be granted extra time to allow for slow processing. Some students may be allowed to work on a laptop or have someone read the paper to them. There are no hard and fast rules and the examination board has the final say, depending on the advice they receive from the educational psychologist or specialist teacher.

*'The question said, "... without reference to Mussolini". Only I read it as, "... **with** reference to". Needless to say, I didn't do very well.' (Annie, aged 16)*

This is not about dyslexic students cheating or getting off lightly. It is simply allowing the dyslexic person the opportunity to do justice to his ability in a subject. If someone does not have the knowledge, then no amount of extra time will help them acquire it. But if a dyslexic student has the knowledge, the special arrangements will allow him to do his best.

Staying calm
Some air and exercise and talking with a friend will help you stay calm and keep exam worries in perspective.

Self-esteem and dyslexia

To have self-esteem means to have respect for ourselves and to value ourselves. In a society where much score is put on educational achievement, it's sometimes easy for people who may not do well at school to think of themselves as not as good as others.

It's important to remember that academic success is just one aspect of our lives. Everybody, whether they are dyslexic or not, has things that they are good at. We also have other areas in our lives which we find more difficult. For example, some people find they have a natural ability at running, or cooking, drawing or mathematics. Some people find that they are good with animals and others might be skilled with technical equipment, whilst others shine at ball games.

Different skills
We all have strengths and weaknesses. What are your strengths?

Yet the person who can make delicious meals may not be able to catch a ball. In many cases, this doesn't matter. We often choose to ignore the areas where we struggle and concentrate on developing our skills. If one of our weaker areas is literacy, however, it's not that easy to simply ignore it. It can have a huge impact on a person's everyday life. Because so little has been understood about dyslexia until relatively recently, many dyslexics have believed, from their early school days, that they are lazy or stupid. As a result, they often don't think very highly of themselves. In cases like this, it's even more important to find something that they can do well and develop it.

From strength to strength
Using and developing our strengths builds our self-esteem.

It's very important that we all learn to value people for who they are and what they can do, rather than criticizing or making fun of them for the things that they find difficult. Literacy is just one of many thousands of skills that humans have acquired over the centuries and, if technology progresses at its present rate, we may have little need for reading and writing by the next century. Perhaps then it will be the dyslexic, 'top-down', creative thinkers who will be amongst the most respected people in society. Who knows?

Resources

Organizations and websites

British Dyslexia Association (BDA)
98 London Road, Reading RG1 5AU

Helpline: 0118 966 8271
e-mail: info@dyslexiahelp-bda.demon.
co.uk

Admin: 0118 966 2677
e-mail: admin@bda-dyslexia.demon.
co.uk

Website: www.bda-dyslexia.org.uk

Information and advice on dyslexia. The Helpline has contacts across the world.

Dyslexia International Tools and Technologies (DITT)
Rue Defacqz 1,
B-100 Brussels, Belgium

Tel.:   02 537 7066

Europe's Children – Our Concern
Rue Washington 40,
B-1050 Brussels, Belgium

Tel.:   02 537 48 36

Information in English, French, German and Spanish.

European Dyslexia Association (EDA)
Tel.:   +41 52 2 202 1707
Fax: +41 52 2 202 1712

EDA has 39 member associations in 24 European courntires.

International Dyslexia Association (IDA)
8600 LaSalle Road, Chester Bldg Suite 382,
Baltimore, MD 21286-2044, USA

Tel: 410-296-0232
Fax: 410-321-5069

IDA has branches in each US state and members in 60 countries around the world.

World Dyslexia Network Foundation (WDNF)
Tel: 020 8770 0888

WDNF has contacts around the world.

Recommended reading

Help for the dyslexic adolescent
by E. G. Stirling
Available from 114, Westbourne Road,
Sheffield S10 2QT
Tel: 0114 266 2286
Tips on reading, spelling, handwriting,
study skills and exams as well as some
first-hand experiences from students who
are dyslexic.

Use your Memory by Tony Buzan
Published by BBC Books
ISBN 0-563-53730-2
Techniques for improving memory.

Music & Dyslexia – Opening New Doors
edited by T. R. Miles and John Westcombe
Published by Whurr Publishers
ISBN 1-86156-205-5
First-hand accounts from dyslexic
musicians.

Basic Topics in Mathematics for Dyslexics
by Anne Henderson and Elaine Miles
Published by Whurr Publishers
ISBN 1-86156-211-X
Suggestions for teachers and students on
making maths understandable.

The Mind Map Book by Tony Buzan
Supplied by Technicolor
ISBN 0-56353732-9
Mind Mapping® is the registered trade-
mark of The Buzan Organization 1990.

The Buzan Centre Ltd (Europe)
54 Parkstone Road, Poole, Dorset BH15 2PG
Tel: 01202 674676

Videos and multimedia

Language shock – Dyslexia across cultures
DITT multimedia pack including a written
guide, a website and a 28-minute BBC video
on which young dyslexics across Europe
speak for themselves.

Get Ahead with Lana Israel. Island World
Video. ISBN 5-022366 100816
A students' guide to Mind Mapping®, with
an introduction by Tony Buzan.

Sources used in this book

T. R. Miles and John Westcombe, *Music & Dyslexia – Opening New Doors*, Whurr Publishers (2001). Quote on page 41 by Jacob, aged 11.

www.bda-dyslexia.org.uk (British Dyslexia Association website; 'Successful Dyslexics', May 2001; 'Life as a Dyslexic Student', March 2001)

Dyslexia International Tools and Technologies website including the article by Dr Harry T. Chasty, 'What is Dyslexia?'

Dyslexia Institute website including the article by Liz Brooks 'Dyslexia: 100 years on Brain Research and Understanding'

International Dyslexia Association website; factsheet #976-01/00 'Testing for Dyslexia'

US Learning Disability website

Glossary

anomaly — something which is different from the 'normal'.

auditory — about sounds.

concept — an idea.

concept cards — cards which show how similar concepts are connected, using colour to link groups of ideas together.

decoding — reading by breaking down words into sounds and syllables.

dictation — when one person speaks and another writes down what they have said exactly as they have said it.

dominant — stronger. Describes something that has control over something else, such as 'the dominant hemisphere' – the side of the brain which takes control.

dyscalculia — a developmental condition which affects the way some people process information about numbers and maths.

dyslexia — a developmental condition which affects the way some people process sounds and written language.

encoding — spelling by building up words sound by sound and syllable by syllable.

gene — the part of a chromosome that contains the chemical instructions about which features we inherit from our parents.

genetics — the study of genes and chromosomes.

hemisphere — one half of a globe shape. A hemisphere of the brain is one side of the brain.

kinesthetic — to do with physical movement.

laterality — right- or left-handedness. Knowing right from left.

lateral thinking — the ability to think about situations or problems in a different or unusual way.

linear — along a line.

literacy — reading and writing.

long-term memory — the part of our memory that we use to recall information or experiences from the past. For example, being able to remember events from childhood.

multisensory teaching — a method of teaching which uses several senses at once: seeing, hearing, saying, feeling.

neurological — to do with the nervous system and the brain.

numeracy — ability to understand numbers and mathematical ideas.

phonology — the processing of sounds in spoken language.

short-term memory — the part of our memory that we use to to recall information that has been given to us recently. For example, remembering a list of instructions.

spatial awareness — understanding how things are, or how things fit together, in a given space.

structured learning — learning in a logical way that builds up gradually on the patterns that have already been learned.

syllable — a part of a word which contains one vowel sound and can be heard as a 'beat' of a word: mag/net, tel/e/vi/sion, etc.

Index